# The Best of

Secret Recipes for Making the Tastiest Dips

BY: Valeria Ray

## License Notes

Copyright © 2019 Valeria Ray All Rights Reserved

All rights to the content of this book are reserved by the Author without exception unless permission is given stating otherwise.

The Author have no claims as to the authenticity of the content and the Reader bears all responsibility and risk when following the content. The Author is not liable for any reparations, damages, accidents, injuries or other incidents occurring from the Reader following all or part of this publication.

# A Special Reward for Purchasing My Book!

Thank you, cherished reader, for purchasing my book and taking the time to read it. As a special reward for your decision, I would like to offer a gift of free and discounted books directly to your inbox. All you need to do is fill in the box below with your email address and name to start getting amazing offers in the comfort of your own home. You will never miss an offer because a reminder will be sent to you. Never miss a deal and get great deals without having to leave the house! Subscribe now and start saving!

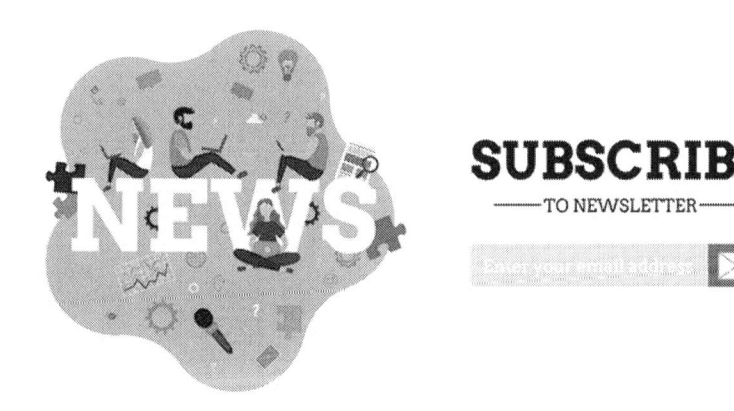

https://valeria-ray.gr8.com

# Contents

Easy and Delicious Dips Recipes ............................................. 7

(1) Berry Good Dip .................................................................. 8

(2) Basic Salsa ........................................................................ 10

(3) Edamame Dip .................................................................... 13

(4) Roasted Pumpkin Dip ....................................................... 15

(5) Peanut Butter Chocolate Chip Dip ................................. 17

(6) Baba Ghanoush Dip/Spread ............................................ 19

(7) Pumpkin Dip ...................................................................... 21

(8) Tzatziki ............................................................................... 23

(9) Fruit Dip ............................................................................. 25

(10) Artichoke Hearts ............................................................. 27

(11) Honey Ricotta Dip .......................................................... 30

(12) Onion Dip ......................................................................... 32

(13) Low Carb Cookie Dough Dip ........................................ 34

(14) Carrot Hummus .......................................................... 36

(15) Strawberry Fruit Dip ................................................... 38

(16) Vegetarian Dips .......................................................... 40

(17) Cheesecake Dip .......................................................... 42

(18) Dill Dip ...................................................................... 44

(19) Peanut Butter Cheesecake Dip ................................... 46

(20) Cheese and Herb Dip .................................................. 48

(21) Walnut Chocolate Fruit Dip ........................................ 50

(22) Tomatillo Salsa ........................................................... 53

(23) Queso ........................................................................ 55

(24) Pico De Gallo ............................................................. 57

(25) Layered Mediterranean Dip ....................................... 59

(26) Bean Dip .................................................................... 62

(27) Tirokafteri ................................................................. 64

(28) Guacamole ................................................................ 67

(29) 7 Layer Dip ................................................................ 69

(30) Corn Salsa ................................................................. 71

About the Author ................................................................. 73

Author's Afterthoughts ....................................................... 75

# Easy and Delicious Dips Recipes

MMMMMMMMMMMMMMMMMMMMMMMMMMMMM

# (1) Berry Good Dip

This recipe utilizes the deliciousness of frozen strawberries and fat-free cream cheese.

**Makes:** 16

**Preparation Time:** 15 mins.

**List of Ingredients:**

- Strawberries (8 oz, frozen)
- Cream cheese (4 oz, softened, fat-free)
- Sour cream (¼ cup, fat-free)
- Sweetener (1 tablespoon, granulated)

**Direction:**

1. In a blender add the strawberries and process until smooth.

2. Beat the cream cheese into a small bowl with a handheld mixture until smooth.

3. Mix in the sour cream, sugar and strawberry; stir until thoroughly combined.

4. Place in the refrigerator until ready to serve.

## (2) Basic Salsa

Exquisite spicy delight made with three hot peppers and other ingredients.

**Makes:** 18

**Preparation Time:** 25 mins.

**List of Ingredients:**

- Tomatoes (8 cup)
- Onions (2½ cup)
- Peppers (1 ½ cup, green)
- Pepper (1 cup)
- Garlic (6 cloves)
- Cumin (2 teaspoons)
- Pepper (2 teaspoons)
- Vinegar (1/3 cup)
- Sweetener (1/3 cup, granulated)
- Tomato sauce (15 oz)
- Tomato paste (12 oz)
- Salt (1/8 cup, canning)

MMMMMMMMMMMMMMMMMMMMMMMMMMMMMMMM

**Methods:**

1. Wash, peel and deseed the various ingredients and chop all the vegetables and place into a pot.

2. Add the spices and the other remaining ingredients and cook over medium heat until boiling.

3. Lower heat and slowly boil for approximately 10 minutes.

4. Pour into jars and seal canning jars and continue cooking in a hot water bath for a minimum of 10 minutes.

# (3) Edamame Dip

This Edamame dip is magnificent, it's delicious taste and nutritious contents is just splendid.

**Makes:** 8

**Preparation Time:** 30 mins.

**List of Ingredients:**

- Edamame (1 ½ cup, shelled, frozen)
- Water (½ cup)
- Onion (¼ cup, red)
- Cilantro (3 tablespoons, fresh)
- Vinegar (2 tablespoons, rice)
- Olive oil (1 tablespoon)
- Salt (½ teaspoons)
- Beans (16 oz, white, drained)
- Garlic sauce (1 ½ chili)

**Methods:**

1. Firstly, thaw out the edamame and then cook it before shelling it.

2. Next drain the can of white beans and set aside.

3. In a food processor add all the ingredients and blend on low until smooth.

4. Pour the dip into a serving bowl, secure and refrigerate for a couple of hours before serving.

## (4) Roasted Pumpkin Dip

A simple five ingredient dip recipe that is sure to leave you speechless.

**Makes:** 10

**Preparation Time:** 45 mins.

**List of Ingredients:**

- Pumpkin (1 butternut)
- Cumin (1 teaspoon, ground)
- Peanut butter (2 tablespoons, crunchy)
- Chili sauce (¼ oz)
- Olive oil

**Methods:**

1. In the oven roast the pumpkin at 350-degrees Fahrenheit until soft and tender, approximately 30 minutes.

2. Scoop out the flesh from inside of the pumpkin and mash it.

3. Add the ground cumin, chili sauce and peanut butter, to the mashed pumpkin and stir to mix well.

4. Drizzle in some olive oil and stir again.

# (5) Peanut Butter Chocolate Chip Dip

A scrumptious Peanut Butter Cup Dip filled with delicious chocolate chips.

**Makes:** 18

**Preparation Time:** 15 mins.

**List of Ingredients:**

- Cream cheese (8 oz, softened)
- Peanut butter (½ cup, sugar-free)
- Stevia (¼ cup)
- Chocolate chips (¼ cup, dark, mini)

MMMMMMMMMMMMMMMMMMMMMMMMMMMMMMM

**Methods:**

1. In a mixing bowl place all the ingredients and mix until thoroughly combined.

2. The mixture will be a smooth consistency.

# (6) Baba Ghanoush Dip/Spread

This delicious spread is simple to make and will be make you the life of the party.

**Makes:** 6

**Preparation Time:** 40 mins.

**List of Ingredients:**

- Eggplant (3 lbs.)
- Olive oil (3 tablespoons)
- Tahini (1/3 cup)
- Garlic (2 cloves)
- Lemon juice (½ cup)
- Salt and pepper to taste

MMMMMMMMMMMMMMMMMMMMMMMMMMMMMMMM

**Methods:**

1. Use the olive oil to rub the outside of the eggplant and place into a roasting pan.

2. Roast for a minimum of 20 minutes at 450 degrees and skins will be charred and inside will be tender.

3. Deseed and peel the eggplant once it has cooled and chop up the insides and place into a food processor.

4. Add the crushed garlic, tahini, salt, pepper, and lemon juice and mix on low speed until coarse paste forms.

5. You can add a few tablespoons of water to help thin out the mixture some.

# (7) Pumpkin Dip

This is a very delicious and creamy pumpkin dip that is normally served with graham crackers.

**Makes:** 16

**Preparation Time:** 10 mins

**List of Ingredients:**

- Cream cheese (8 oz, fat-free)
- Pumpkin (½ cup, canned)
- Seasoning mix (2 tablespoons, taco)
- Garlic powder (1/8 teaspoons)
- Bell pepper (½ cup, chopped)

MMMMMMMMMMMMMMMMMMMMMMMMMMMMMMMMM

**Methods:**

1. Beat together the first four ingredients using a hand mixer until smooth

2. Mix in the bell pepper and chill until ready to serve.

# (8) Tzatziki

Tzatziki is a rich sauce commonly served with grilled meats or as a dip. Tzatziki is made with tofu mixed with cucumber, vinegar, lemon juice, garlic, salt and olive oil.

**Makes:** 4

**Preparation Time:** 2 hrs. 30 mins.

**List of Ingredients:**

- Tofu (12 oz, box, silken)
- Lemon juice (3 tablespoons)
- Vinegar (1 tablespoon, white, wine)
- Garlic (2 cloves)
- Salt (½ teaspoons)
- Olive oil (2 tablespoons)
- Cucumber (1, deseeded, grated)

MMMMMMMMMMMMMMMMMMMMMMMMMMMMMMMM

**Methods:**

1. Add tofu, salt, vinegar and lemon juice to a blender and mix until smooth.

2. Add chopped garlic and oil and mix some more. Pour mixture into a serving bowl.

3. Squeeze excess water out of cucumber with hands and add to dip.

4. Stir gently, add any fresh herbs, and stir again.

5. Place in fridge and chill for 2 hours before serving.

## (9) Fruit Dip

This Fruit dip is not just delicious but it's also extremely nutritious exquisitely made by two simple ingredients.

**Makes:** 15

**Times:** 10 mins.

**List of Ingredients:**

- Heavy cream (10 oz)
- Yogurt (1 cup)

MMMMMMMMMMMMMMMMMMMMMMMMMMMMMM

**Methods:**

1. Whip the heavy cream using a handheld mixer, until thickened.

2. Add in the yogurt and stir to mix well.

3. Chill in the refrigerator until ready to serve.

# (10) Artichoke Hearts

If you're a fan of Artichoke, try this tasty Artichoke Hearts recipe full packed with essential nutrients and minerals.

**Makes:** 4

**Preparation Time:** 15 mins.

**List of Ingredients:**

- Onion (½, yellow)
- Artichoke hearts (8 oz, marinated)
- Spinach (12 oz, frozen, chopped)
- Olive oil (1 tablespoon)
- Tofu (12 oz, silken, firm)
- Vinegar (2 tablespoons, apple cider)
- Garlic (3 cloves)
- Yeast (½ cup, nutritional)
- Basil (1 teaspoon, dried)
- Parsley (1 teaspoon, dried)
- Pepper (¼ teaspoons, cayenne)
- Salt (1 teaspoon)
- Pepper (½ teaspoons)

MMMMMMMMMMMMMMMMMMMMMMMMMMMMMMM

**Methods:**

1. Sauté the spinach, artichoke hearts and onion over medium high heat for approximately 6 minutes, ensure onions become soft.

2. Place the tofu, yeast, garlic, vinegar, and various spices into a blender and mix until smooth.

3. Pour mixture into a bowl and mix in the spinach mixture. Mix well.

4. Pour the mixture into a non-stick baking dish and bake at 350 degrees for a minimum of 20 minutes.

# (11) Honey Ricotta Dip

This Honey Ricotta Dip is delightful, it has a magnificent taste and a wonderful texture.

**Makes:** 18

**Preparation Time:** 20 mins

## List of Ingredients:

- Cheese (1 cup, ricotta)
- Milk (1 tablespoon, of choice)
- Honey (2 teaspoons)
- Vanilla extract (1 teaspoon)

## Methods:

1. In a mixing bowl combine all the ingredients together and beat until well combined.

# (12) Onion Dip

This Onion Dip is the ideal substitute for sour cream, when added to your chips completely boost the flavor.

**Makes:** 8

**Preparation Time:** 20 mins.

**List of Ingredients:**

- Macadamia nuts (2 cups)
- Water (¾ cups)
- Sea salt (1 teaspoon)
- Garlic (1 clove)
- Onion (1 cup)

MMMMMMMMMMMMMMMMMMMMMMMMMMMMMMM

**Methods:**

1. Soak the macadamia nuts in water for approximately several hours to help soften them.

2. Drain the water from the soften macadamia nuts, and place into a blender along with the water, garlic and sea salt, and blend until smooth.

3. Pour into a bowl and fold in onions and gently mix. Place into the refrigerator to chill.

# (13) Low Carb Cookie Dough Dip

This Low Carb Cookie Dough dip will instantly become your favorite because of its extravagant taste and low carbs.

**Makes:** 14

**Preparation Time:** 15 mins.

**List of Ingredients:**

- Yogurt (8 oz, of choice)
- Protein powder (1 scoop)
- Sweetener (1 tablespoon, granulated)
- Flour (1 tablespoon, coconut)
- Chocolate chips

**Methods:**

1. Mix together the yogurt, protein powder and sweetener in a mixing bowl until well combined.

2. Add in the coconut flour a little at a time while continuously stirring. Only add enough coconut flour to reach your preferred consistency.

3. Sprinkle the chocolate chips on top and serve.

# (14) Carrot Hummus

Creamy, delicious and heathy that is three out of a thousand words I can say about this fantastic Carrot Hummus.

**Makes:** 14

**Preparation Time:** 15 mins.

**List of Ingredients:**

- Carrots (1 cup, grated)
- Chickpeas (1 cup, cooked)
- Lemon juice (2 tablespoons)
- Tahini (2 tablespoons)
- Onions (2 green)
- Olive oil (1 tablespoon)

**Methods:**

1. Add the chickpeas, onions, lemon juice, olive oil, and tahini to a food processor. Mix until you reach at a smooth consistency.

2. Add a small portion of the water if you are having problems with the consistency.

3. Gently mix in the carrots (grated) and serve.

# (15) Strawberry Fruit Dip

A simple, delicious and easy to make Strawberry Fruit Dip made with only five ingredients.

**Makes:** 16

**Times:** 15 mins.

## List of Ingredients:

- Strawberries (1 cup, sliced)
- Sour cream (¼ cup)
- Sweetener (1 tablespoon, granulated)
- Vanilla (¼ teaspoons)
- Whipping cream (½ cup)

## Methods:

1. Blend together the sour cream, strawberries, vanilla and sugar in a blender until smooth.

2. Beat the cream in a small bowl until peaks form.

3. Fold the whipped cream into strawberry mixture.

4. Cover and place into the refrigerator for approximately 1 hour.

# (16) Vegetarian Dips

This delicious dip is perfect for vegetarians.

**Makes:** 10

**Preparation Time:** 30 mins.

**List of Ingredients:**

- Red peppers (7 oz, jar roasted)
- Cream cheese (½ cup, fat-free)
- Scallions (2)
- Garlic (1 clove)
- Lemon juice (1 tablespoon)

**Methods:**

1. In a blender, add all the ingredients and process until thoroughly pureed.

2. Pour into a bowl and chill for roughly 2-3 ½ hours before serving.

3. Enjoy!

# (17) Cheesecake Dip

This Cheesecake Dip is super creamy, completely addicting and rich in taste and as a bonus it is so easy to make!

**Makes:** 10

**Preparation Time:** 15 mins.

## List of Ingredients:

- Sour cream (1 cup)
- Cream cheese (½ cup)
- Whey protein (¼ cup, vanilla)
- Vanilla extract (2 teaspoons, sugar-free)
- Swerve (2 tablespoons)

## Methods:

1. Place all the ingredients into a mixing bowl and mix until thoroughly combined.

# (18) Dill Dip

Easy to make, simple and delicious, this Dill dip is perfect for your snacks or crackers.

**Makes:** 8

**Preparation Time:** 30 mins.

**List of Ingredients:**

- Sour cream (1 cup, sour cream)
- Mayonnaise (½ cup)
- Dill weeds (1 tablespoon)
- Parsley flakes (1 tablespoon)
- Onion (1 tablespoon, minced)
- Celery (½ teaspoons, seeds)
- Garlic (1/8 teaspoons, powder)
- Salt (¼ teaspoons, seasoning)

MMMMMMMMMMMMMMMMMMMMMMMMMMMMMMMM

**Methods:**

1. In a medium sized bowl place all the ingredients and stir well.

2. Place the dip in the fridge to chill for several hours before serving.

# (19) Peanut Butter Cheesecake Dip

Try this delicious Peanut Butter Cheesecake Dip for Deliciousness on the go.

**Makes:** 12

**Preparation Time:** 20 mins.

**List of Ingredients:**

- Cream cheese (8 oz, softened)
- Peanut butter (1 ½ cup, unsweetened)
- Butter (½ cup)
- Vanilla extract (1 teaspoon)
- Salt (¼ teaspoons)
- Stevia (1 teaspoon, vanilla, liquid)

**Methods:**

1. Allow the butter and the cream cheese to come to room temperature.

2. Place all the ingredients into a bowl or stand mixer and mix together until thoroughly combined. The mixture should be at a smooth consistency.

3. Can taste and adjust sweetener.

# (20) Cheese and Herb Dip

Have you been looking for healthy ways to eat your cheese, well you're in luck try this tasty Cheese and Herb Dip.

**Makes:** 6

**Preparation Time:** 20 mins.

## List of Ingredients:

- Sour cream (½ cup)
- Cream cheese (¼ cup)
- Goat cheese (¼ cup)
- Chives (2 tablespoons)
- Parsley (1 tablespoon)
- Tarragon (1 tablespoon)
- Garlic (1 clove)

MMMMMMMMMMMMMMMMMMMMMMMMMMMMMMM

## Methods:

1. In a blender place all the ingredients and blend until smooth.

2. Season and Taste with salt and pepper, if desired.

3. Pour into serving bowl, secure, and chill for a couple of hours before serving.

# (21) Walnut Chocolate Fruit Dip

Walnut Chocolate Fruit Dip is a sweet twist on the savory snacks or crackers.

**Makes:** 10

**Preparation Time:** 20 mins.

**List of Ingredients:**

- Walnuts (1 cup)
- Dates (6)
- Cocoa (2 tablespoons)
- Nectar (2 tablespoons, agave)
- Vanilla extract (1 teaspoon)
- Olive oil (2 tablespoons)
- Water (3 tablespoons)

MMMMMMMMMMMMMMMMMMMMMMMMMMMMMMM

**Methods:**

1. Soak the dates in some water for approximately several hours to help soften them up.

2. Chop the walnuts finely in a food processor, you want a fine ground.

3. Add the dates to the walnuts one at a time and thoroughly grind the dates.

4. Add the cocoa, sweetener, and vanilla and continue processing on low.

5. Slowly add a small portion of oil and then water. Alternate between the two until you have reached the desired consistency.

# (22) Tomatillo Salsa

Hot and spicy delicious Tomatillo Salsa perfect for tortilla chips.

**Makes:** 18

**Preparation Time:** 30 mins.

**List of Ingredients:**

- Tomatillos (6 cup, chopped)
- Onions (3 cup, chopped)
- Peppers (3, jalapeno)
- Garlic (6, cloves)
- Cilantro (½ cup)
- Lemon juice (½ cup)
- Cumin (2 teaspoons)
- Salt (1 tablespoon)
- Pepper (1 teaspoon)

MMMMMMMMMMMMMMMMMMMMMMMMMMMMMMM

**Methods:**

1. Chop the onions, peppers, garlic, tomatillos and cilantro. Once chopped, place everything into a large pot over high heat and frequently stir until boiling.

2. Reduce the heat and simmer for a minimum of 20 minutes.

3. Ladle into pint sized jars and process in a hot water bath to store for future use or you can refrigerate for immediate use.

# (23) Queso

Queso is a delicious appetizer or side dish consisting of flour, melted margarine and salsa.

**Makes:** 16

**Preparation Time:** 30 mins.

**List of Ingredients:**

- Flour (¼ cup, unbleached)
- Yeast (¼ cup, nutritional)
- Salt (1 teaspoon)
- Paprika (1 teaspoon)
- Garlic powder (½ teaspoons)
- Margarine (2 tablespoons, fat-free)
- Salsa (1 cup)
- Water (1 cup)

MMMMMMMMMMMMMMMMMMMMMMMMMMMMMMM

**Methods:**

1. Place all the dry ingredients into a small saucepan and then add the water.

2. Constantly whisk the mixture over medium heat until thoroughly combined.

3. Add the salsa and margarine and continue whisking for an additional two more minutes.

## (24) Pico De Gallo

Pico De Gallo is a delicious Mexican dip that Is authentic, nutritious and tasty.

**Makes:** 9

**Preparation Time:** 30 mins.

**List of Ingredients:**

- Tomatoes (3, large)
- Onion (½ cup)
- Garlic (2 garlic)
- Peppers (2 jalapeno)
- Cilantro (3 tablespoons)
- Olive oil (1 tablespoon)
- Lime juice (1 tablespoon)

MMMMMMMMMMMMMMMMMMMMMMMMMMMMMMM

**Methods:**

1. Firstly, core the tomatoes and deseed.

2. When finished remove the seeds from the jalapeno peppers.

3. Finely chop the onions, tomatoes, and cilantro and mince the garlic and jalapenos.

4. Mix all the ingredients together in a mixing bowl and allow to sit for approximately 15 minutes.

# (25) Layered Mediterranean Dip

This delicious dip is brilliant for the Mediterranean cuisine lovers.

**Makes:** 12

**Preparation Time:** 20 mins.

**List of Ingredients:**

- Cream cheese (8 oz, fat-free)
- Cheese (1 ¼ cup, feta)
- Milk (2 tablespoons, of choice)
- Basil (1 tablespoon, dried)
- Spinach (10 oz, frozen)
- Tomato (1)
- Onions (3 green)
- Olives (¼ cup, sliced, black)

MMMMMMMMMMMMMMMMMMMMMMMMMMMMMMM

**Methods:**

1. Firstly, allow the cream cheese to soften and crumble the feta cheese.

2. Next, thaw and drain the spinach.

3. Beat together the softened cream cheese, Feta cheese (1 cup), milk, and basil until well blended.

4. Spread the mixture out on the bottom of a 9-inch pie pan.

5. Spread the spinach, green onions, tomato (chopped), and the sliced olives on top and sprinkle with the remaining feta cheese.

6. Cover and refrigerate for approximately 1 hour before serving.

# (26) Bean Dip

This bean dip is easy to whip up and extremely tasty.

**Makes:** 5

**Preparation Time:** 20 mins.

**List of Ingredients:**

- Edamame (1 ½ cup, shelled)
- Salsa (1/3 cup)
- Onion (1, green)
- Cilantro, (2 tablespoons, fresh, leaves only)
- Seasoning (¼ teaspoons, Mexican)

**Methods:**

1. Cook and de-shell the frozen edamame.

2. Place all the ingredients into a food processor and blend until smooth.

## (27) Tirokafteri

A time efficient, easy to make and delicious Tirokafteri sure to leave your taste buds tingling.

**Makes:** 12

**Preparation Time:** 25 mins.

**List of Ingredients:**

- Cheese (2 cups, feta)
- Pepper (1, hot)
- Vinegar (1 tablespoon)
- Olive oil (4 tablespoons)
- Oregano (½ teaspoons)

MMMMMMMMMMMMMMMMMMMMMMMMMMMMMMMM

**Methods:**

1. Firstly, in a small bowl place the feta cheese and add some water.

2. When finished, allow to sit for approximately one hour and drain and cut the cheese into cubes.

3. Next grill the pepper and cut open. Deseed and then chop pepper into pieces.

4. In a mixing bowl, place the cheese cubes along with the pepper pieces.

5. Use an electric mixer to beat the peppers and cheese together.

6. Add the vinegar and slowly add the olive oil while you are mixing.

7. Stir in the oregano and serve.

# (28) Guacamole

A delicious, homemade and fresh Guacamole awaiting your chips.

**Makes:** 4

**Preparation Time:** 20 mins.

**List of Ingredients:**

- Avocado (1, large)
- Tomatoes (2, plum)
- Onion (½)
- Cilantro (¼ cup)
- Pepper (1, jalapeno)
- Lime juice (1 tablespoon)
- Salt (½ teaspoons)
- Pepper (¼ teaspoons)

**Methods:**

1. Firstly, cut the avocado into halves and remove pit.

2. Scrape the pulp from each half and place into a small bowl.

3. Use a fork or potato masher and coarsely mash the pulp together.

4. Add the remaining ingredients and gently stir until just combined.

## (29) 7 Layer Dip

Spice up your chips with this tasty, zesty and delicious 7-layer dip.

**Makes:** 10

**Preparation Time:** 15 mins.

**List of Ingredients:**

- Beans (16 oz, refried)
- Taco Seasoning/Mexican Seasoning
- Sour cream (1 cup)
- Guacamole (1 cup)
- Salsa (1 cup)
- Lettuce (1 cup)
- Cheese (1 cup)
- Olives (4 oz, sliced)
- Tomatoes (1 cup)

**Methods:**

1. Gather all the ingredients and find a baking dish that will allow you to create seven separate layers.

2. Mix together the beans with the Mexican/taco seasoning.

3. Layer the dip in this order: beans, sour cream, guacamole, salsa, lettuce, cheese, olives, and tomatoes.

## (30) Corn Salsa

This Corn Salsa Is perfect for family get together and reunions.

**Makes:** 25

**Preparation Time:** 35 mins.

**List of Ingredients:**

- Kernel corn (15 oz, whole)
- Green pepper (½ cup)
- Bell pepper (12 cup, red)
- Onion (½ cup, red)
- Tomatoes (2)
- Olives (¼ cup, black)
- Peppers (2 tablespoons, pickled, jalapeno)
- Pepper juice (1 teaspoon, pickled, jalapeno)
- Wine vinegar (2 tablespoons, red)
- Salt (½ teaspoons, garlic)
- Pepper (½ teaspoons)

MMMMMMMMMMMMMMMMMMMMMMMMMMMMMMM

**Methods:**

1. Firstly, chop up all the vegetables and drain and rinse the corn.

2. Next, place all the ingredients into a mixing bowl and mix well.

3. Cover and place in the refrigerator for several hours to chill.

# About the Author

A native of Indianapolis, Indiana, Valeria Ray found her passion for cooking while she was studying English Literature at Oakland City University. She decided to try a cooking course with her friends and the experience changed her forever. She enrolled at the Art Institute of Indiana which offered extensive courses in the culinary Arts. Once Ray dipped her toe in the cooking world, she never looked back.

When Valeria graduated, she worked in French restaurants in the Indianapolis area until she became the head chef at one of the 5-star establishments in the area. Valeria's attention to taste and visual detail caught the eye of a local business person who expressed an interest in publishing her recipes. Valeria began her secondary career authoring cookbooks and e-books which she tackled with as much talent and gusto as her first career. Her passion for food leaps off the page of her books which have colourful anecdotes and stunning pictures of dishes she has prepared herself.

Valeria Ray lives in Indianapolis with her husband of 15 years, Tom, her daughter, Isobel and their loveable Golden Retriever, Goldy. Valeria enjoys cooking special dishes in her large, comfortable kitchen where the family gets involved in preparing meals. This successful, dynamic chef is an inspiration to culinary students and novice cooks everywhere.

# Author's Afterthoughts

Thank you for Purchasing my book and taking the time to read it from front to back. I am always grateful when a reader chooses my work and I hope you enjoyed it!

With the vast selection available online, I am touched that you chose to be purchasing my work and take valuable time out of your life to read it. My hope is that you feel you made the right decision.

I very much would like to know what you thought of the book. Please take the time to write an honest and informative review on Amazon.com. Your experience and opinions will be of great benefit to me and those readers looking to make an informed choice.

*With much thanks,*

*Valeria Ray*

Printed in Great Britain
by Amazon